W9-BRW-698

THINGS TO MAKE YOU HAPPY

LISA M. GERRY

NATIONAL
GEOGRAPHIC
KiDS

WASHINGTON, D.C.

FOREWORD

Dear Reader,

As the director of **the Happiness Project,** which explores the art and science of being happy, I have been investigating "happiness" for **20 years.**

In every country, and in every culture, when people are asked what they want, **the most popular answer is happiness.** And when parents are asked what they most want for their children, the answer is also happiness. **Everyone wants to be happy.**

People often ask me, **What is the secret to happiness?** One secret is, **Don't wait to be happy!** Happiness doesn't magically come to you through things you can buy or something you can own; **it's a state of mind** that already exists in you. The secret to happiness is to start **by doing things that make you happy.**

Doing things that make you happy is **good for your physical** and **mental health.** Scientists have described laughter as **"stationary jogging,"** because a good laugh gives you many of the same benefits as physical exercise. And smiling **releases brain chemicals** that help you feel calm and peaceful.

Being happy helps you **feel confident,** make friends, be optimistic, and go out and explore life.

This book will help you **be true to yourself,** discover talents and strengths, and live a life you love. This is the purpose of happiness—to help you **embrace who you are and enjoy every moment of your precious, one-of-a-kind life!**

ROBERT HOLDEN, PH.D.
AUTHOR OF *HAPPINESS NOW!* AND *BE HAPPY*

The secret to happiness is to start by doing things that make you happy.

① HAVE A BELLY LAUGH

Check out these jokes submitted by our very own *NG Kids* readers.

7

Q How do you make a tissue dance?

A Put a little boogie in it.

Paige, age 7, California

A man walks into the doctor's office.

Man: Doctor, doctor, I've had a dream, and I don't know what it means!

Doctor: What happened in the dream?

Man: There was a door with a sign on it, and no matter how hard I pushed, the door wouldn't open.

Doctor: What did the sign say?

Man: Pull.

Bethany, age 11, Tennessee

PULL

Q How does NASA organize a party?

A They planet.

Sebastian, age 14, Maine

Knock, Knock.
Who's There?
Water.
Water who?
Water you doing? Let me in!

Holland, age 12, New Jersey

Q What do you call a cow that can't fly?

A Ground beef.

Jude, age 10, Illinois

Q Why did the can crusher quit his job?

A Because it was soda pressing!

Maura, age 12, Texas

Q What phone does a turtle like to carry?

A A shell phone.

Isabel, age 9, Maryland

get silly!

Playtime is still in session!

Channel your inner little kid and pick up some crayons, Play-Doh, or a Slinky.

3 GET MOVIN

G!

FIND A HEART-PUMPING, SWEAT-INDUCING ACTIVITY THAT YOU LOVE

SO, YOU'VE HEARD ABOUT THESE THINGS CALLED ENDORPHINS, RIGHT? They're chemicals that your brain releases that make you feel happy! There are actually activities you can do (and even foods you can eat!) to encourage your body to release more of them. One awesome way to get your body to release endorphins (as well as other positive compounds) is to do aerobic exercise—like running, jumping, or dancing—for at least 20 to 30 minutes. So, find an activity that you love to do and set a goal to do it at least three days a week.

NEED SOME MORE IDEAS? HOW ABOUT THESE
▼HAPPY ACTIVITIES ...

- ROLLER-SKATE
- PUNCH A PUNCHING BAG
- RIDE A BICYCLE
- PLAY BASKETBALL
- JUMP ROPE
- SWIM
- PLAY TAG, KICKBALL, OR CAPTURE THE FLAG
- HAVE A DANCE PARTY
- TRY MARTIAL ARTS, LIKE KARATE OR TAE KWON DO
- JUMP ON A TRAMPOLINE

4

When sea otters hunt for food, they often wrap their babies up in kelp so that they don't float away.

⑤ SMILE!

EVEN IF YOU'RE NOT FEELING PARTICULARLY JOYFUL,

"turning that frown upside down" might also turn your mood around! A study found that just the act of smiling might reduce feelings of stress in certain situations. And smiling is a great way to make other people feel happier and more at ease.

> "Peace begins with a smile."
> – Mother Teresa

Meditate

5 Awesome Facts About Meditation:

1. Meditation is a practice to train and quiet the mind.

2. Studies have found that after eight weeks of meditating daily, people experience neuroplasticity, which means their brains physically change. So cool!

3. Meditation has been shown to lower physical pain, anxiety, and blood pressure as well as boost memory, alertness, and creativity.

4. Meditation is not about clearing or ridding your mind of thoughts; in fact, thoughts are a normal part of practicing meditation. As the doctor, author, and meditator Deepak Chopra said, "Meditation is not a way of making your mind quiet. It is a way of entering into the quiet that is already there—buried under the 50,000 thoughts the average person thinks every day."

5. Meditation isn't a religious practice—many people of all different faiths meditate.

"None but ourselves can free our minds."
– Bob Marley

6

10 Famous Meditators

1 Oprah Winfrey

Jerry Seinfeld **2**

3 Jim Carrey

Michael Jordan **4**

5 *Paul McCartney*

Katy Perry **6**

7 *Ellen DeGeneres*

Derek Jeter **8**

9 *Russell Simmons*

George Lucas **10**

⑦ KEEP
AN OPEN MIND

When you're willing to see things from a different angle, cool things start happening—you meet interesting people, make amazing discoveries, and embark on awesome adventures.

"Only the development of compassion and understanding for others can bring us the tranquility and happiness we all seek." – *Dalai Lama*

8

There's a ROLLER COASTER at the WASHUZAN HIGHLAND PARK in Japan called the SKY CYCLE where riders propel themselves by PEDALING ON BICYCLES more than

52 FEET

(15.8 m)

ABOVE THE GROUND.

9

LEARN *to* love THE WAY YOU LOOK

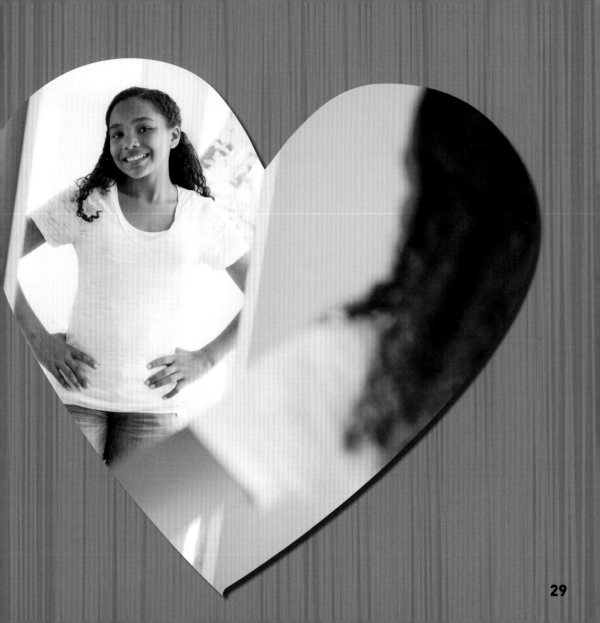

OUR BODIES ARE
PRETTY INCREDIBLE.

THEY HELP US JUMP HIGH, RUN FAR, DANCE, DO CARTWHEELS, AND CREATE AMAZING ART, AND THEY CAN SOMETIMES EVEN DO COOL, WEIRD TRICKS THAT MAKE PEOPLE LAUGH (LIKE WIGGLING OUR NOSTRILS!). BUT SOMETIMES WE MIGHT FEEL LIKE THAT'S NOT ENOUGH, THAT ON TOP OF ALL OF THAT COOL STUFF, WE'D BE HAPPIER IF WE LOOKED A CERTAIN WAY. THAT'S NOT ACTUALLY THE CASE, THOUGH. INSTEAD, ONE WAY TO BE HAPPIER IS TO DEVELOP A POSITIVE, HEALTHY BODY IMAGE. SO, WHAT IS THAT, EXACTLY?

"Positive body image is not just feeling good about our appearance, it's feeling good about our bodies overall—how we feel inside, how our bodies work, and what they can do," says Lindsay Kite, Ph.D., who co-founded the nonprofit foundation Beauty Redefined with her twin sister. "People with a positive body image use their bodies as instruments rather than as objects."

So no matter what our teeth, hair, noses, arms, legs, or stomachs look like, let's make a pact to appreciate who we are and love our bodies for what they can DO. Let's take that energy we spent wishing we could change our bodies and use it to change the world!

LINDSAY SHARES
5 WAYS TO
BOOST OUR BODY IMAGE:

1 Be aware of negative media messages. Remember that often the media is trying to sell us something. One way to do that is by first trying to make us feel like something is wrong with our bodies so that we will be more likely to buy whatever they're selling to fix it. So, ask yourself: Who is sending this message? How do they hope I feel after seeing it? Instead of feeling bad about yourself, pause. Then say, I see what you're trying to do, but I'm not going to fall for it.

2 Use your body as an instrument rather than as an ornament to decorate the space you're in. Do this by joining a sports team, setting an exercise goal, singing, painting, skateboarding, or playing guitar. It's incredibly empowering to know that your body is a tool you can use rather than just something to be looked at.

3 Make a list of the parts of your body you appreciate and all the ways your body is working well. We can lose sight of the awesome things our bodies are capable of when we're so focused on what our bodies look like.

4 Redefine what it means to have a great body. Instead of worrying about what other people might think about the way you look, create your own definitions of what it means to be happy, healthy, and successful.

5 Watch how you talk about your body. When you stop saying negative things about your body, it actually helps you stop thinking those things. Even better? Say the goal out loud by telling friends and family to stop speaking negatively about your and other people's bodies. Who knows? You might even inspire them to make positive changes too!

31

10 Pic Flow

k
ers

(though not from your neighbor's garden)!

SOMETHING YOU LOVE

11

PASSION, OR A FEELING OF INCREDIBLE ENTHUSIASM,

is what propels artists to create master-pieces, scientists to make discoveries, and humanitarians to selflessly help others. It's the feeling that you care so deeply about something that you'll push onward even when the going gets tough.

Marine biologist and National Geographic young explorer **DASH MASLAND** felt passionately about the **OCEAN** from a very young age and has made exploring it as well as conserving it **HER LIFE'S WORK.**

WHEN DID YOUR LOVE OF NATURE AND MARINE BIOLOGY BEGIN?

I grew up on the coast of Maine, U.S.A., and my family and I spent a lot of time exploring beaches and tide pools. We had a little boat that we'd use to putter around Casco Bay. As a kid, being on the water really inspired me, and literally for as long as I can remember, I've wanted to be a marine biologist.

WHEN DID YOU BEGIN WORKING TOWARD IT AS A CAREER?

I did my first snorkeling camp when I was in fifth grade, and then I got certified to scuba dive when I was 15. In high school, I spent a semester at sea, and when I was 18, I went off and did an expedition in Honduras, studying coral reefs. In college, I was 100 percent on the marine biology track. My passion to get on the water—and then to get under it—really drove me from a young age.

WHAT IS IT ABOUT THE OCEAN THAT'S SO FASCINATING TO YOU?

I think that when you look out over the ocean and think about what's under there, with a vivid imagination, the possibilities are limitless. I'm a person who's always looking out expecting to see something huge jump out. I'm always scanning for whales or dolphins or other animals to appear. The ocean is so striking and beautiful—you really can imagine this whole other world beneath the surface that's open to explore.

WHAT ARE YOU WORKING ON RIGHT NOW?

I'm working on a project studying what Hawaiian monk seals eat. We are interested in their diet because seals like to eat fish, and so do humans. So we want to figure out a way that humans and seals both have enough to eat.

HOW DO YOU FIND OUT WHAT THE SEALS ARE EATING?

Well, we can't watch what they're eating because they're underwater. We have to figure out what they eat based on what comes out the other end. We can look in their poop for fish, but sometimes not all the bones show up, because they dissolve in the stomach during the digestive process. What I'm doing is looking for fish DNA in the seal poop to see what they're eating.

WHEN DID YOU BECOME INTERESTED IN SEALS?

Where I grew up in Maine, there are lots of harbor seals that haul out on the rocks. One of our favorite things to do was to get into our little boat and look for seals.

HOW DOES PASSION PLAY A ROLE IN WHAT YOU DO?

It can be challenging to make a career out of something you love, but the way I feel when I'm standing next to the ocean—that passionate feeling in my heart—is what keeps me on track. Also, Hawaiian monk seals are one of the most endangered species of seal in the world. The fact that what I'm studying could have a true, applied effect to help save a species is an amazing feeling.

Check out these adorable

INSTA-SMILE

WHO: Finchen and Rabbit
WHAT: Deer and rabbit
WHY THEY'LL MAKE YOU HAPPY: The two buds met in a field on a farm and have stuck together ever since. They alert each other if ever there's danger or a predator nearby, and since Finchen is too big to join the sweet bunny in his bed underground, the rabbit built a grassy nest, big enough for the two of them, where they both sleep.

WHO: Augie and Suzy
WHAT: Dog and chimpanzee
WHY THEY'LL MAKE YOU HAPPY:
When Suzy's mother passed away, Augie stepped in to help care for her. Suzy climbs on Augie like a jungle gym, rides on his back, and feeds the pooch jelly sandwiches after he's eaten all his food. If ever Suzy gets scared, she runs right to Augie, her best friend.

—and furry!—best friends.

WHO: Tonda and T.K.
WHAT: Orangutan and cat
WHY THEY'LL MAKE YOU HAPPY: When Tonda was separated from her mate, she was very sad and lost interest in playing—and even painting, her favorite hobby. But then she met T.K., and all was right with the world. Tonda carried the kitty all around, fed him, petted him, and dangled toys for him to play with. Pretty soon, Tonda was back to her old, art-loving self.

FRIENDS COME IN ALL SHAPES AND SIZES.

INSTA-SMILE

NEVER FEAR, LITTLE PIG. I'LL PROTECT YOU!

WHO: Saimai and piglets

WHAT: Bengal tiger and pigs

WHY THEY'LL MAKE YOU HAPPY: In the wild, pigs would likely be prey for a tiger, but at the Sriracha Tiger Zoo in Si Racha, Thailand, these little piglets were raised with Saimai, and they've become the best of pals. They clean one another, take naps together, and even snuggle together.

FRIENDS—
AND FOOD!—
ARE THE WAY TO
MY HEART.

WHO: Cleo and Sterling
WHAT: Dog and duck
WHY THEY'LL MAKE YOU
HAPPY: At first, Cleo
didn't want to be friends,
but Sterling, the deter-
mined duck, followed him
everywhere he went. Now
they play in the pond
together, explore the tall
grass in the backyard,
share meals, and even
sleep in the same kennel.

I CAPTURED
HIS HEART!

13

WATCH
YOUR

FAVORITE
TV SHOW
OR MOVIE

Discover A HOBBY you Love

15

Find a group of people who

If you're wild about, say, video games, it's fun to have someone to talk to about them, swap tips, and play together. So whatever you're into— whether it's dog training, creative writing, or environmentalism—find people who like what you like and get together to talk, laugh, learn, and play!

HERE ARE A FEW WAYS TO MEET SOME NEW FOLKS WHO SHARE YOUR INTERESTS.

Take a class. Do you love to act, make pottery, or play guitar? Enroll in a class (check out your local community center!) with other people your age.

Start a group or a club. Want to meet other people who love to garden or write code? Post flyers around your school, church, or neighborhood, and meet up once a week to talk shop.

enjoy doing what you enjoy

Spread the word. Do you love restoring old clocks? The more people you talk to about your interests, the more likely you are to meet someone who knows someone else who's interested in that too.

Go to an event. Check the newspaper or Internet for local meet-ups—like a drum circle or comic book signing—and go with your parents, or a trusted adult, to ones that interest you. There you'll meet other people who like that sort of thing too!

THE WORLD'S LARGEST
GINGERBREAD HOUSE
WAS BUILT IN BRYAN, TEXAS,
U.S.A. IT STOOD
62 FEET (18.9 m)
BY **42 FEET.** (12.8 m)
THE BUILDERS USED
22,304 PIECES OF CANDY!
TALK ABOUT A SUGAR RUSH!

16

GET
ORGANIZED

"If you **can't find your home- work,** you don't know where the notes are that you need to study, **or you can't remem- ber the date an assignment's due,** all of that **creates stress,"** says Kathy Jenkins, professional organizer and founder of the Organizing Tutor. "But by being organized, you can alleviate that stress, and you'll have more time to do the things you want to do!"

17

CHECK OUT

1 Have a place for everything, and keep everything in its place. What causes a lot of clutter for people is when they get something but don't know where to put it—they just set it down anywhere. So the first time you get something that doesn't yet have a place, make a decision as to where you're going to put items like that from here on out. Then, at the end of every day, make sure everything is put away where it's supposed to be.

2 Have an active and long-term paper management system. Find out what sort of system works best for you for keeping your daily papers and notes organized. For some students, it's a binder with pocketed dividers; for many, it's an expandable folder; whereas for others, it's a spiral notebook and a single folder for handouts. When deciding on a system, think about what has worked best for you in the past and what will be easiest for you to upkeep. Have another container to keep at home—a magazine box or a desktop file box—where you can store papers from previous semesters that you might need for exams.

3 Have a family calendar as well as a personal planner. I recommend that families keep a paper calendar in a central location in the house, like the kitchen. Each family member should update the calendar with his or her after-school activities, chores, events, etc. Then pick a night, once a week, to sit down with the family and go over the upcoming week. In addition, you should have a personal planner where you write down all of your homework as well as all of your extracurricular activities.

18

Be resilient. Nev

er, ever give up!

"Success consists of going from failure to failure without loss of enthusiasm." – Winston Churchill

19

Make a list of things you like about you!

THINGS I LIKE ABOUT ME:

- My curly hair
- I like to laugh
- The way I dance
- The funny freckles on my hand
- I'm nice to people
- I'm so tall, I can help smaller people reach things
- I'm good at crafting
- My family and friends
- I'm a good listener
- How my eyes look just like my mom's and sister's

"Our true nature is not some ideal that we have to live up to. It's who we are right now, and that's what we can make friends with and celebrate." – Pema Chödrön

INSTA-SMILE

20

TILLMAN

When this feisty English bulldog was an eight-week-old puppy, he discovered his favorite toy—a skateboard. Now, at eight years old, he is still crazy for riding and can even flip the board and ride up and down ramps. He can also snowboard, wakeboard, and surf!

These three adorable pooches aren't your average lapdogs. In fact, they're more like
SUPER PUPS!

PUDSEY

This dancing dog (a cross between a border collie, bichon frise, and Chinese crested) won *Britain's Got Talent* with his owner and trainer, Ashleigh. He's also the star of an upcoming movie, *Pudsey: The Movie.*

RICOCHET

This sweet golden retriever was being trained as a service dog when she decided she would much rather be surfing. Now, she combines surfing with service and rides waves with kids with disabilities, helping them keep their balance on the board. So cool!

21

HELP who

One of the best ways to be happy is by helping other people and making them happy. Here are some ideas to get you started ...

1 Visit an elderly relative or family friend.

2 Give someone a compliment. Be genuine and specific.

PEOPLE
need it

3 Stand up for someone who's being teased or bullied.

4 Volunteer! Anywhere from a homeless shelter or health charity to a nature center!

5 Practice random acts of kindness. See an opportunity to make someone's day better? Do it!

EMBRACE YOUR WEIRD!

Sometimes sticking out in a crowd can feel uncomfortable, but it's the things that make us different that also make us special. And, very often, it's the funny little quirks and interests that people have when they're young that become awesome talents and passions as they grow up. So spend some time today focusing on what makes you unique rather than just like everyone else. **If you need some inspiration, think about what the talented actress Emma Stone once said when accepting an MTV Movie Award for being a trailblazer.**

"I hope that you'll find your trailblazers ... [and] that you'll continue to harness your own originality and what makes you unique, because I know that when you're a teenager—and even sometimes when you're an adult—what sets you apart can feel like a burden, and it's not. A lot of the time, it's what makes you great." — *Emma Stone*

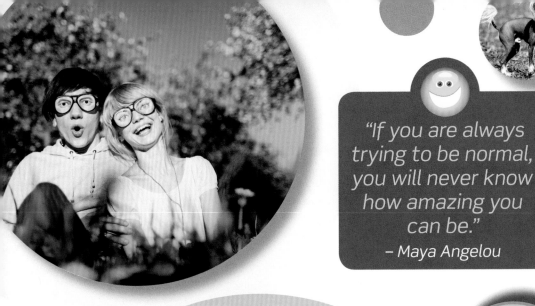

"If you are always trying to be normal, you will never know how amazing you can be."
– Maya Angelou

22

63

LISTEN TO MUSIC

23

STUDIES HAVE FOUND THAT MUSIC CAN LESSEN ANXIETY, RELIEVE STRESS, AND BOOST LISTENERS' MOODS. SO TURN UP THOSE HAPPY TUNES!

CHECK OUT THESE 5 MOOD-BOOSTING SONGS:

1. **"HAPPY,"** Pharrell Williams

2. **"DON'T WORRY, BE HAPPY,"** Bobby McFerrin

3. **"FIREWORK,"** Katy Perry

4. **"ON THE SUNNY SIDE OF THE STREET,"** Billie Holiday

5. **"HAKUNA MATATA,"** *The Lion King*

I'M ON MY WAY! I'LL BE THERE IN A JIFF!

An adorable Pomeranian named Jiff holds the world record for the fastest dog on two legs. And he holds the record for both his hind legs (10 meters/32.8 ft in 6.56 seconds) and his front legs (5 meters/ 16.4 ft in 7.76 seconds). **HE'S SUPERCUTE AND SPEEDY!**

24

25

EXPRESS
YOUR FEELINGS

Bottling up your feelings can make you even more sad, mad, or scared. It's important—and healthy!—to let your feelings flow through you. Here are five ideas for how to let it all out.

1 Write it all down in a journal, or make a list of everything you're feeling.

2 Tell a friend or family member about what's going on.

3 Draw a picture of how you're feeling.

4 Release that pent-up energy by exercising, laughing, or crying.

5 Listen to a song that expresses how you feel. Play it loud and sing along.

SELF-TALK IS THE WAY WE TALK TO OURSELVES, ABOUT OURSELVES.
It's the little voice in our heads that either says something positive and uplifting, like "You can do it!," or something mean and negative, like "You're never going to make this goal." And it turns out, our thoughts, and the words we choose to talk about ourselves, have a HUGE impact on how we feel and even how we perform.

"Friendship with oneself is all-important, because without it one cannot be friends with anyone else in the world."
– Eleanor Roosevelt

5 TIPS FOR IMPROVING YOUR SELF-TALK

1 RECOGNIZE HOW YOU TALK TO YOURSELF. The first step toward turning an inner bully into a BFF is paying attention to your thoughts.

2 WHEN YOU CATCH YOURSELF NAME-CALLING, or saying something negative, like "You can't even___," "You aren't ___ enough," or "You won't be able to ___," picture a stop sign, and silence that negative talk.

3 WHEN YOU START DOWN A NEGATIVE SELF-TALK SPIRAL, turn it around by thinking of all the things you did well today, what you did right, what you like about yourself, and why everything is going to be okay.

4 WHEN SOMETHING GOES WRONG, OR YOU'RE FEELING DOWN, think of what you would say to a best friend or your sibling and say the same things to yourself.

5 THINK OF A PHRASE THAT MAKES YOU FEEL HAPPY AND HOPEFUL, and in times of stress, repeat it to yourself. If you're having trouble thinking of one, try one of these:
- I am stronger than I think.
- It might not feel like it now, but I will feel better soon.
- I am very loved.
- I can do this.
- I will learn from this challenge and be stronger for it.

BE TRUE TO YOURSELF

"Your time is limited, so don't waste it living someone else's life ... Don't let the noise of others' opinions drown out your own inner voice. And most important, have the courage to follow your heart and intuition." – Steve Jobs

TWEET!

I THOUGHT I RECOGNIZED THAT CHIRP!

Chicks **begin** communicating even before they hatch. They actually chirp back and forth to their brothers and **sisters from** inside their **shells!**

eat choc

licorice

29

It doesn't take a scientist to tell us that chocolate makes us happy, but it turns out scientists can tell us why it does. Chocolate contains compounds that release endorphins—or happy-making chemicals—in our brains. The delicious dessert also has properties that make us feel focused and relaxed. Need more convincing? Here, give it a try (and a taste!).

HOW TO MAKE CHOCOLATE CUPCAKES

Get a parent's help to create a batch of these sweet treats.

1. Preheat the oven to 350°F. Line 12 muffin cups with paper liners.

2. Beat 1 cup of butter, 1½ cups of sugar, 1 cup of unsweetened cocoa powder, 1 teaspoon of baking powder, ½ teaspoon of baking soda, and ¼ teaspoon of salt in a large bowl with a mixer for 1 minute.

3. Add 2 large eggs and beat them for 2 minutes. Beat in 1 cup of milk and 2 teaspoons of vanilla, and then add 2½ cups of flour.

4. Spoon about ¼ cup of batter into each muffin cup, filling each about ⅔ full. Bake them for 20 to 25 minutes.

5. Repeat step 4 with the remaining batter. Let the cupcakes cool for 5 minutes before frosting.

30 PLAY WITH a puppy

There's actually a chemical reason you feel happier after snuggling a sweet pooch. When a person pets a dog, a hormone called oxytocin is released. It is a chemical that helps lower blood pressure and reduce stress.

Be an awesome

31

teammate

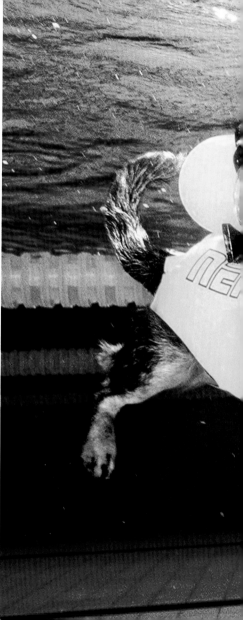

Imagine diving deep beneath the ocean's surface and seeing all kinds of cool marine life, like jellyfish, octopuses, barracuda, and dogs—wait, what? Dogs? Yep! There are dogs—and even a cat!—that use custom-made tanks and masks to go scuba diving!

32

GET A GOLDFISH

AND FOR TEN MINUTES, DO NOTHING BUT WATCH IT SWIM

Surround **yourself** with **34** **colors** that make **you** happy

Check out what Angela Wright, renowned color psychologist and author of *The Beginner's Guide to Colour Psychology*, has to say about

how colors affect how we feel.

Q: CAN COLOR INCREASE FEELINGS OF HAPPINESS?

Yes, absolutely. There was a recent study where they had some participants work in offices with no color—just gray, white, and black—and then others work in offices with color. Overwhelmingly, people worked better, were more productive, and were happier when surrounded by colors.

Q: WHAT COLORS MAKE MOST PEOPLE FEEL HAPPY?

If a color is light and somewhat bright, it will likely improve someone's mood. But the real key to making someone feel happy is to use harmonious colors. People are actually born with a strong instinct for these harmonies, and it has contributed to our survival throughout evolution. When nature wants to warn you of danger, there are usually slightly disharmonious colors present. The classic danger signal in the natural world is black and warm yellow (think bees!).

Q: WHAT ARE SOME EXAMPLES OF HOW DIFFERENT COLORS MAKE US FEEL DIFFERENTLY?

There are four psychological primaries: red, blue, yellow, and green.

• Red is the color of the body, it has a physical effect on us. Red is stimulating and can raise our pulse rate and blood pressure. Some people perceive red as exciting and exhilarating, whereas others perceive it as aggressive or as a strain.
• Blue affects the mind, and all of its hues will stimulate an intellectual response.
• Yellow affects the observer's emotions, like their ego and self-confidence.
• Green restores the balance between the mind, the body, and the emotions.

Q: ARE THERE ANY COLORS THAT MAKE EVERYONE HAPPY?

Not exactly. Every person has a special bond with one of these four color groups. However, the good news is, if all the colors in a color scheme (like in a bedroom or classroom) are drawn from the same color group, they will create harmony, and harmony is attractive to everyone. Also, as a rule of thumb, reds, oranges, and yellows tend to lift the spirits, whereas blues and purples calm the mind.

35

Dance IN THE RAIN

36

Seahorses like to swim in pairs, with their tails linked together. AWWW.

37

APPRECIATE SIMPLE **PLEASURES**

Take a bubble bath, watch the sun set, or eat a warm cookie.

What makes **YOU HAPPY?**

38

Rice Krispies Treats?

Jumping on the trampoline?

Reading comic books?

Make a "Happy List" of all the things that lift your spirits and refer to it when you need **a pick-me-up.**

"One of the secrets of a happy life is continuous small treats." — Iris Murdoch

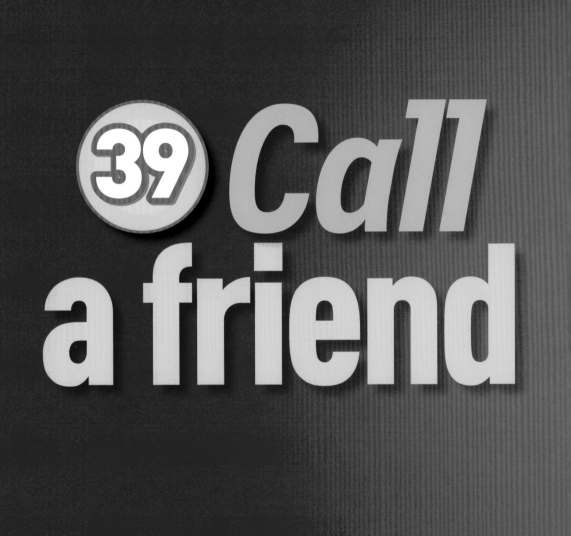

39 Call a friend

While most people stick to building snowmen, three brothers from New Brighton, Minnesota, U.S.A., have mastered the art of creating SNOW SCULPTURES of sea creatures. They've sculpted an enormous SHARK, WALRUS, and a PUFFER FISH, and most recently, they spent several weeks building a giant sea turtle measuring 12 FEET (3.7 m) tall, 37 FEET (11.3 m) long, and 31 FEET (9.4 m) wide.

SO COOL!

41

BE KIND TO OTHERS

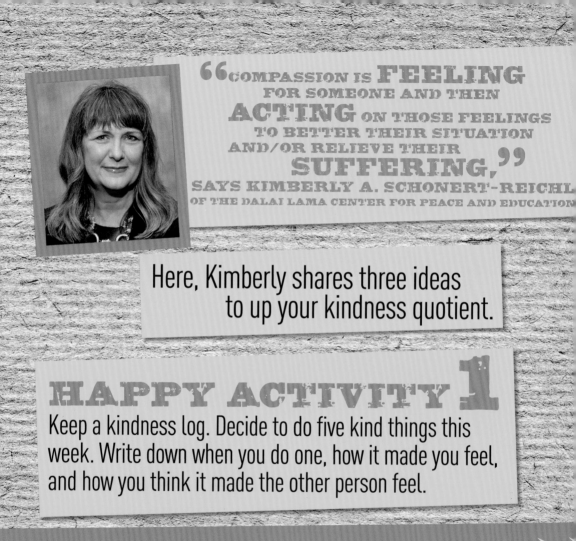

"COMPASSION IS **FEELING** FOR SOMEONE AND THEN **ACTING** ON THOSE FEELINGS TO BETTER THEIR SITUATION AND/OR RELIEVE THEIR **SUFFERING,**" SAYS KIMBERLY A. SCHONERT-REICHL OF THE DALAI LAMA CENTER FOR PEACE AND EDUCATION

Here, Kimberly shares three ideas to up your kindness quotient.

HAPPY ACTIVITY 1

Keep a kindness log. Decide to do five kind things this week. Write down when you do one, how it made you feel, and how you think it made the other person feel.

Being kind toward others can have many benefits. Here are just a few: ➤

HAPPY ACTIVITY 2

Create a kindness club. Gather a group of friends and be kind together. Volunteer at a local retirement home, raise money for a homeless shelter, or be the welcoming committee for new kids at school.

HAPPY ACTIVITY 3

Make a kindness collage. Collect news stories and pictures of people being kind—from magazines, newspapers, or the Internet—and glue them on a poster board. Hang it somewhere where you'll see it every day to inspire you and remind you of the power of kindness.

- More confidence
- Lower cholesterol
- Lower risk of heart disease
- Greater self-esteem
- A strong support system of friends
- Lower stress
- Better mood
- Inspire kindness in others

42

Set.
aside

FAMILY TIME

Put
43
PeR

Fect
to rest

Many trees grow each year from **NUTS** that squirrels forgot they **BURIED.**

make YOUR

"IF YOU WANT TO CHANGE THE WORLD, START OFF BY MAKING YOUR BED," SAID U.S. NAVY ADMIRAL WILLIAM H. McRAVEN, A TOP NAVY SEAL. He was speaking to a group of graduates at the University of Texas, U.S.A. He went on to say, "If you make your bed every morning, you will have accomplished the first task of the day. It will give you a small sense of pride, and it will encourage you to do another task, and another, and another. And by the end of the day, that one task completed will have turned into many tasks completed."

BED

45

Keep a

Record your thoughts,

(They're definitely worth remembering!)

journal

feelings, ideas, and dreams.

46

GET CREATIVE

1. Write a short story about your life.
2. Use something old to make something new.
3. Redecorate your bedroom.
4. Paint a self-portrait.
5. Create a new recipe with your favorite foods.

INSTA-SMILE

There are
CAT CAFÉS
in Paris
and Japan
where
kitties roam
around
inside for
you to pet
and play
with while
you enjoy
your coffee.

Look
AT PICTURES OF
CUTE
ANIMALS

Not only will it make you happy, but a study in Japan found that looking at pictures of cute baby animals may also boost your attention to detail and overall work performance. Win-win!

Be
CURIOUS.

"All life is an experiment. The more experiments you make, the better." – *Ralph Waldo Emerson*

50

CURIOSITY IS THAT ITCH IN YOUR GUT THAT GETS YOU ASKING QUESTIONS AND LOOKING FOR ANSWERS. IT'S AN INTERNAL COMPASS LEADING YOU TOWARD THE SUBJECTS THAT INTEREST YOU, AND IT'S HOW DISCOVERIES ARE MADE AND PASSIONS ARE FUELED. GREG GOLDSMITH, A TROPICAL ECOLOGIST AND NATIONAL GEOGRAPHIC YOUNG EXPLORER, EXPLAINS HOW SCIENCE AND CURIOSITY GO HAND IN HAND, WHERE HIS LOVE OF NATURE HAS LED HIM, AND HOW HIS DESIRE TO HELP OTHERS MOTIVATES HIM TO EXPLORE.

WHEN DID YOUR LOVE OF NATURE BEGIN?

For as long as I can remember, I have loved being outdoors and exploring. I loved the sense of independence that comes with relying on a map, a compass, and your own two feet to get from one place to another.

WHEN DID YOU REALIZE YOU WANTED TO MAKE TROPICAL ECOLOGY YOUR CAREER?

Well, first I realized that science was a great excuse to be outdoors, and to be exploring and discovering. Then I came to the realization that you really can't understand the world's diversity without going to the tropics. What's so fascinating about the tropics is just how little we know about the diversity that's there.

WHAT ARE YOU WORKING ON NOW?

I study how the climate affects how tropical forests function— what kinds of plants grow, how fast they grow, what happens when there's a drought, what happens when it's warmer or colder. I'm trying to understand how climate change will affect their fate in the future.

WHERE DO YOU DO MOST OF YOUR WORK?

In the past five to seven years, I've spent about three or four months a year in some part of the tropics. Last year, I went to 13 countries, but primarily, I've been working in Brazil, Peru, and Costa Rica.

DO YOU HAVE A FAVORITE PLACE TO WORK?

Oh, yeah, that's an easy one. My absolute favorite places on the planet are what are called tropical montane cloud forests. They're forests that are often immersed in a layer of clouds that extends all the way down to the ground. They're one of the rarest ecosystems on the planet, and they are incredibly beautiful. They're also well known for their high biodiversity—there are lots of things that occur there that don't occur anywhere else on the planet.

HOW DOES CURIOSITY PLAY A ROLE IN WHAT YOU DO?

Curiosity is wanting to know more about things that interest you. And for some reason, I've always wanted to know more about what's around the next corner. Being a scientist and a tropical ecologist has allowed me to see new places, meet new people, eat unusual food, learn new languages, and do things that I've never done before. So this job, to me, just couldn't get any better.

WHY IS CURIOSITY IMPORTANT?

As an ecologist, the knowledge that we're trying to gain is driven by a desire to leave the world a better place. We can't conserve and preserve what we don't know about. I'm convinced that there are answers to very hard problems—cures for diseases, better ways to clean water, whatever it might be—that exist in plants, animals, and places that we haven't found yet.

129

TAKE A *nap*

51

INSTA-SMILE

Okuno Shima in Japan is called "RABBIT ISLAND" because of the hundreds of rabbits that have taken over the island.

52

Now, tourists visit the island to FEED THE RABBITS and PLAY WITH THEM.

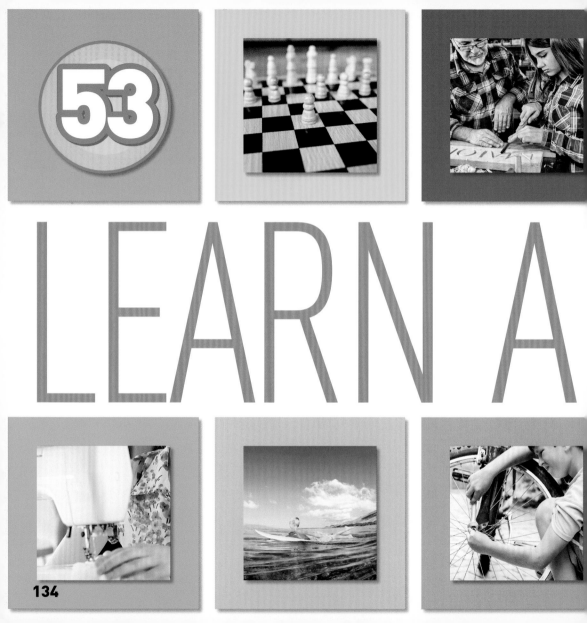

53

LEARN A

SKILL

54

CELEBRATE INTERNATIONAL DAY OF HAPPINESS

The United Nations proclaimed it to be March 20, so mark your CALENDAR!

"Most people are about as happy as they make up their minds to be." – Abraham Lincoln

55

TRY Yoga

Janna Delgado and **Angela Wilson** of the **KRIPALU CENTER FOR YOGA AND HEALTH** explain what yoga is, how it can make **us happier,** and how to **get started.**

Happy Activity Try this yoga pose, cat-cow, to get started and pump up your happiness.

STEP 1: To begin the pose, get down on your hands and knees. Place your hands right underneath your shoulders on the floor and your knees beneath your hips. Spread your fingers out nice and wide.

STEP 2: Inhale deeply and arch your back. Then pull your shoulders down while you look up at the ceiling so that your whole spine has a beautiful arch to it.

STEP 3: As you breathe out, round your back, spread out your shoulder blades, and look toward your belly.

WHAT IS YOGA?

Yoga is a practice that brings together our body, breath, and mind so that these different parts of us are all working together.

HOW CAN PRACTICING YOGA MAKE YOU HAPPY?

Mentally, yoga helps to reduce stress, improve mood, and lower anxiety, and it can help you react less to anger. Physically, yoga helps with flexibility, strength, and balance. Practicing yoga can also be incredibly empowering.

WHEN SHOULD YOU PRACTICE YOGA?

It's good to practice regularly, so rather than having one long session once a week, just try to do a little something every day. The more routine it is, the better, and the more results you'll see.

HOW SHOULD YOU GET STARTED?

There are tons of online resources, DVDs, classes, and books that are geared toward different age groups. Grab hold of something—anything— and find a place to explore. Approach yoga with a spirit of curiosity and playfulness. As you get started, be kind, patient, and compassionate with yourself.

STEP 4: Flow back and forth between these movements three to five times, or however many you like. Make sure you move slowly and breathe fully with each movement.

STEP 5: Check in with yourself to see if anything has shifted or changed. You've gotten oxygen into your system, regulated your breath and nervous system, and set the stage for happiness to unfold.

56

LOOKING FOR YOUR NEXT VACATION DESTINATION?

Check out the hotel in Idaho, U.S.A., shaped like a giant beagle, the Dog Bark Park Inn; Lucy, the six-story-tall elephant in New Jersey, U.S.A., where you can climb a spiral staircase to sit on her back; or the 55-foot (16.7-m)-tall Jolly Green Giant statue in Minnesota, U.S.A.

Welcome to
Blue Earth
Minnesota

143

GIVE SOME
OR HOLD

57

ONE A HUG
SOMEONE'S HAND

So, what is the power of touch, exactly? Well, when you hug someone, or hold their hand, a chemical called oxytocin—which makes people feel happy!—is released in your brain. Touch has also been found to lower blood pressure, boost the immune system, and lower stress. Wow, that deserves a high five or a pat on the back!

BE
GRATEFUL

146

ONE OF THE MOST POWERFUL THINGS YOU CAN DO TO MAKE YOURSELF HAPPIER IS TO PRACTICE GRATITUDE. GRATITUDE IS APPRECIATING ALL THAT IS RIGHT AND GOOD IN YOUR LIFE. AND ONE OF THE GREATEST THINGS ABOUT GRATITUDE IS THAT IT CREATES A HAPPY SNOWBALL EFFECT—THE MORE GRATEFUL YOU FEEL, THE HAPPIER YOU ARE, AND THE HAPPIER YOU ARE, THE MORE GRATEFUL YOU FEEL! SO GET THE SNOWBALL STARTED WITH THESE TWO GRATITUDE-GENERATING ACTIVITIES.

HAPPY ACTIVITY 1:
Keep a Gratitude Journal

Every night, for about five minutes, take time to reflect on your day and all the parts of it that you're thankful for. If you're having trouble thinking of good things, try answering these questions.

1. What went well today?
2. Who are the people in my life I love? What is it about them that I love?
3. What parts of my body are healthy and working well?
4. What makes me laugh?
5. Did I see anything, do anything, or eat anything today that made me smile?
6. What parts of my day and my life bring me comfort?
7. What opportunities do I have to make myself happy?
8. What opportunities do I have to make others happy?
9. Who made today better?
10. What are my skills/talents/gifts/blessings?

HAPPY ACTIVITY 2:
Write a Thank-You Note

You know what's even better than thinking of why you're grateful? Telling someone that you're grateful for them or for something they did. Try writing someone a note, whether it be to a parent, teacher, coach, sister, brother, or friend, and tell them that you appreciate them in your life, and why. Be specific about what it is they do that you're grateful for and how those things make you feel. Not only will you be making whoever you send it to feel happy, you'll feel happier too!

Chimpanzees show
affection like humans.

59

They kiss, hold hands, hug, and even pat one another on the back.

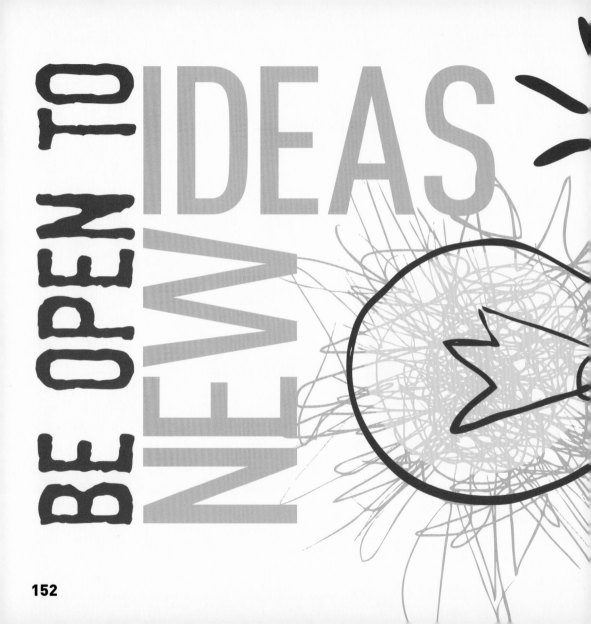

BE OPEN TO NEW IDEAS

breathe!

61

SOUNDS EASY ENOUGH, RIGHT?

Research has found that deep, slow breathing can reduce our stress response and help us calm down. And less stress equals greater happiness! "How you breathe makes a difference in your physical and emotional well-being," says Janna Delgado, yoga teacher and specialist at the Kripalu Center for Yoga and Health. "When you're looking to change how you're feeling, the simplest way to do that is to change how you're breathing."

Here, Janna shares a simple breathing exercise.

1 Find a comfortable place to sit or lie down where you won't be disturbed or distracted for a few minutes.

2 Place one hand on your belly and one on your chest, over your heart region. (Note: This positioning of the hands is calming for many people and can be a very comforting thing to try in your everyday life.)

3 Begin to notice your breath. As you inhale and exhale, notice where you feel it in your body. You might notice your breath moving in and out of your belly, the rising and falling of your chest, or even the air flowing in and out of your nostrils.

4 Begin breathing in and out, through your nose. Take a few moments to **create a slow and comfortable** breathing pattern through your nostrils.

5 Now as you breathe in, let your **belly relax and expand.** As you breathe out, pull your belly button in, pushing all of the air out. Feel your breath moving in your belly for a few moments.

6 Now begin breathing into your **chest/heart as well.** The next time you breathe in, expand your belly with air—and then breathe in a bit more to fill your chest/heart with air too. Then **breathe out and let your chest/heart relax** and release, squeezing your belly button in to push all of the air out. Continue to breathe this way for another few moments.

7 Gently let yourself stop this breathing exercise and **sit quietly** for a moment or two, paying attention to how you feel.

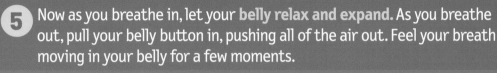

JANNA ADDS, "WITH PRACTICE, YOU WILL NATURALLY START TO BECOME MORE AWARE OF YOUR BREATH, AND THEN YOU CAN USE IT AS A TOOL TO BALANCE YOUR ENERGETIC AND EMOTIONAL STATES."

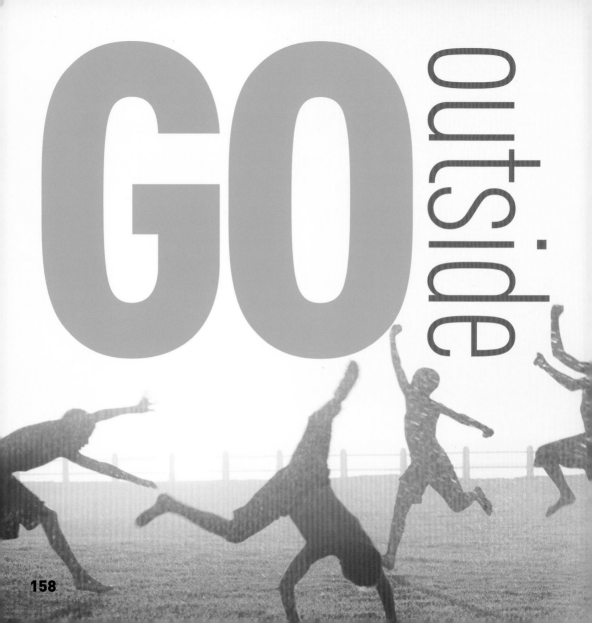

GO outside

Have you ever had a day when you went from your house to the car to school and then back to the house, where you sat in front of the TV or your computer for the rest of the day? At the end of a day like that, you may have felt tired, cranky, and a little down. The thing is, humans need to be outside, in the sunlight, breathing fresh air into our lungs and being inspired by nature. So turn off that glowing screen and step outside!

10 THINGS TO DO OUTSIDE

1. Go for a hike or nature walk.
2. Climb a tree.
3. Roller-skate or in-line skate.
4. Make up a synchronized swimming routine, or play Marco Polo, in a pool.
5. Check out a field guide from the library and try to identify a flower, tree, or bird.
6. Have a water balloon fight.
7. Lay in a hammock.
8. Find a public basketball court and host a half-court tournament.
9. If you live near water, sit and watch the boats go by.
10. Bring a piece of paper and pencil and sketch the scenery.

"Look deep into nature, and then you will understand everything better." – Albert Einstein

63

DON'T BE AFRAID TO *FAIL!*

NOBODY LIKES TO FAIL. It might make us feel sad, frustrated, or even embarrassed. But the truth is, if you dream big and set awesome goals for yourself, you're likely to encounter roadblocks along your way. The key to success is making sure that after you allow yourself a little bit of time to be disappointed, you get back up and try again. The worst thing you can do is to be so afraid you won't succeed that you don't try at all. Not convinced? Check out these five superstars who faced disappointments before they found success.

KATY PERRY

Before she became a pop superstar, Katy was dropped by three record labels.

STEVEN SPIELBERG

Today he may be the Oscar-winning director of movies like *The Adventures of Tintin* and *Jurassic Park*, but he was rejected by the University of Southern California's film school, twice.

OPRAH WINFREY

Now a media mogul and journalist extraordinaire, it's hard to believe that Oprah was fired from her first job as a TV news anchor in Baltimore, Maryland, U.S.A.

THOMAS EDISON

Before Thomas Edison successfully invented the light-bulb, he made thousands of attempts that didn't work.

J. K. ROWLING

When J. K. finished her first book, *Harry Potter and the Sorcerer's Stone*, she sent it to 12 publishing houses—and the book was rejected by all of them.

"It is impossible to live without failing at something, unless you live so cautiously that you might as well not have lived at all—in which case, you fail by default." – J. K. Rowling

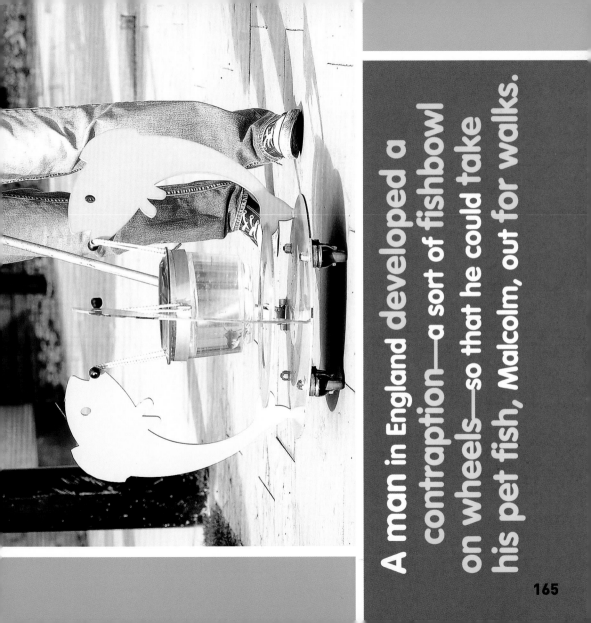

A man in England developed a contraption—a sort of fishbowl on wheels—so that he could take his pet fish, Malcolm, out for walks.

Add a little wonder to your week, or some fairy dust to your day, by mastering a magic trick and performing it for a friend. Chris McCauley, director of education at the Mystery Academy, answers four of our questions and explains a classic trick: how to pull a coin from someone's ear.

Four Questions With Chris McCauley

When did you become interested in magic?

When I was about seven or eight, I got a magic set, and I did magic tricks for my sister. My dad helped me make a floating magic wand, and that was my first trick. It was great.

What is it about magic that's interesting to you?

The goal of magic is to give someone a magical experience. Magic gives children and otherwise powerless people a sort of power that makes them feel special, and it also makes the person who had the magic done for them feel special.

What makes a great magic trick?

I think it's the story and the involvement from the participant. When you're involved in a magic trick, it's much more powerful than seeing one done on TV or in a book. What makes a magic trick great is that personal experience, when someone feels that something magical happened to them.

What tips would you give to someone who's interested in magic?

The most important tip is to focus on one trick instead of a million different things. You want to practice a trick again and again until every little part is correct. Instead of having a bunch of mediocre tricks, a professional magician might only have nine tricks that they do. But they focus on making each piece of those nine tricks perfect.

Coin From Ear

SETUP:

This is the part that you need to do, secretly, in advance.

SETUP STEP 1:

Place a coin on the inside of the second and third fingers of your left hand where your fingers bend. It must be in this exact place.

SETUP STEP 2:

Curl both fingers of both hands. This allows you to grip the edges of the coin with the bend in your fingers without the coin falling and without closing your hand all the way.

SETUP STEP 3:

You should now be able to turn your hands over and rest them in a natural position on the table. Do not clench your hands tightly. The coin is still wedged in the bending area of the fingers of your left hand, but the natural curl of your hands on the table will be enough to keep the coin from falling out of your fingers. If you're standing, hold your hands naturally at your sides, with the backs of your hands pointed toward the audience (the audience must only see the backs of your hands, otherwise they may see the coin from the side). Magicians call this position "finger palm." Now you are ready to perform the trick!

1 Keep the coin in the curve of the fingers on your left hand. Point to the person's ear with your right hand and say, "Excuse me, I think you have something behind your ear!"

2 Pretend to grab something from behind their ear with your right hand.

3 Show the audience that your right hand is empty. They will be expecting something to be in your right hand and will look down at it.

4 Say, "I'm sorry, it's actually over here!" Quickly reach behind their other ear.

5 Mime (or pretend) that you are plucking the coin from behind their ear (really it's been in your hand the whole time). Then show the coin to the audience!

PUT ON YOUR HEADPHONES AND TAKE A TEN-MINUTE DANCE BREAK

THINK HAPPY THOUGHTS

JUST THINKING ABOUT HAPPY EXPERIENCES AND MEMORIES CAN MAKE YOU HAPPIER, SO WHY NOT GIVE THESE SOME THOUGHT?

The last time you laughed really hard.

A time when you made someone else really, really happy.

Something you're looking forward to in the future.

The best meal you've ever eaten.

"Joy is what happens to us when we allow ourselves to recognize how good things really are." – Marianne Williamson

INSTA-SMILE

Many animals—

68

including gorillas, rats, owls, dogs, and penguins—have a laughter-like response when they're tickled.

HAVE

COMPASSION

69

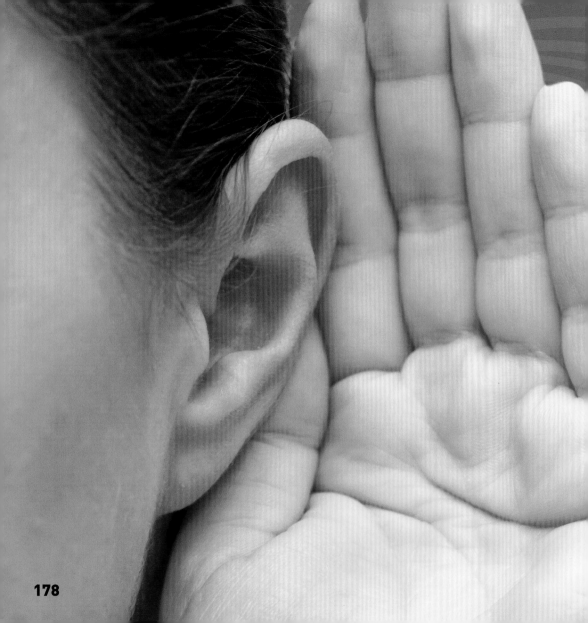

70

BECOME AN AWESOME LISTENER!

Listening is not only a great way to learn new things, it's also one of the best ways to show someone you care about them. Think about it: Who are the people in your life who make you feel special, interesting, and understood? No matter who they are, they're probably great listeners.

AND YOU CAN BE TOO!

Just like with any other skill, the more you practice, the better listener you'll become. So go ahead, listen up!

5 WAYS TO BE A GREAT LISTENER

1 **DON'T INTERRUPT.** Interrupting is a bad habit, and it can make whoever's speaking feel pretty small. No matter **how excited you are** about what someone is saying, **wait until they're done talking** to show your enthusiasm. And even if someone is taking awhile to complete their thought, give them time to **finish their sentence.** Then wait a few seconds more before you respond.

2 **SHOW THAT YOU'RE PAYING ATTENTION.** Nonverbal cues are the messages we communicate with our **body language,** without even having to say anything. When you're listening, show the speaker you care about what they're saying by **sitting up straight,** uncrossing your arms, **making eye contact,** smiling, nodding, and even leaning forward a little.

3 **BE FOCUSED AND PRESENT.** Even if you think you can do two things at once, listening is **best done on its own.** So put away anything that might be distracting, like your phone, book, or video game. Don't doodle or rummage through your backpack. **Just be present and focus** on whoever's talking. The speaker will feel great, and you'll get more from what they're saying.

4 **TRY TO UNDERSTAND.** Instead of thinking about **what you'll say next,** or whether you agree with the speaker, try to listen to what the person is telling you, why it's important to them, and **how it makes them feel.**

5 **ASK FOLLOW-UP QUESTIONS.** When someone is telling a story or sharing their feelings, **don't immediately change the subject** when they stop talking. To show that you're interested, **ask questions** about what they've told you. For example: Then what happened? How did that make you feel? Are you glad you went?

BUILD *something,*
FIX
SOMETHING, OR FIGURE

71

SOMETHING OUT

An eight-year-old boy raised money to pay off overdue lunch balances for kids at his school. When the community caught wind of his efforts, they began donating too, raising more than

$10,000.

72

Take a Whiff

(Try Aromatherapy)

73 Aromatherapy is the practice of using essential oils from plants to improve how a person feels mentally and physically. Here are five mood-boosting scents and how they might affect your happiness.

lavender
Calm, Relaxed, and Sleepy ▼

cinnamon
Mentally Sharp ▼

vanilla
Happy, Joyful, and Relaxed

▼

fresh-cut grass
Relaxed and Joyful

▼

▲

lemon
Energized, Alert, and Less Anxious

74

Sleep soundly

Sleep is the body's way of recharging every night,
and it's very important to your overall health. Sleep increases your ability to learn new things, improves your memory, and boosts your attention span. It also helps you be more alert, keep your emotions steady, and feel happier. With all of sleep's great benefits, it's no wonder experts recommend getting between $8\frac{1}{2}$ and $9\frac{1}{4}$ hours of sleep per night. Here's how to make the most of your shut-eye.

Five Keys to Better Z's

🌙 Turn off TVs, computers, cell phones, and other gadgets at least one hour before bedtime.

🌙 Try to go to sleep and wake up around the same time each day.

🌙 Avoid caffeine after noon each day.

🌙 Exercise regularly.

🌙 Try to decrease stress. If you are feeling anxious, try guided meditation, positive visualization. or a breathing exercise before bed.

TRY
SOMETHING
NEW

INSTA-SMILE

Dogs have been used for many years to assist the blind, but now a new breed of animal has been classified as a potential service animal for people with disabilities— MINIATURE HORSES! While they need more space than many dogs do, they can be housebroken, they follow commands, and they're very calm and good-natured.

77

SET A GOAL AND MAKE A PLAN TO ACHIEVE IT!

Whether your goal is to make a new friend, run a mile, be nicer to your sister, or get an A on your next test, it takes discipline, focus, and motivation to be successful. But when you finish what you set out to do, you will be incredibly proud of yourself and have an awesome sense of accomplishment.

YOU CAN DO IT!

GOAL-SETTING 101

STEP 1: Write your goal down. Place it somewhere you'll see it every day to remind you what you're working toward.

STEP 2: Give yourself a certain amount of time to achieve your goal and write it on the calendar.

STEP 3: Make a plan as to how you can achieve your goal and think about who or what you might need to help you.

STEP 4: Post positive reminders about your goal around your room and home and in your notebooks. For example, Make today count! Don't forget your homework! or Picture the finish line!

STEP 5: When you reach your target date, decide whether you were successful. If you reached your goal, celebrate that victory. If you didn't, celebrate your effort. Then think about what might have contributed to you not reaching your goal, make a new plan, and try again!

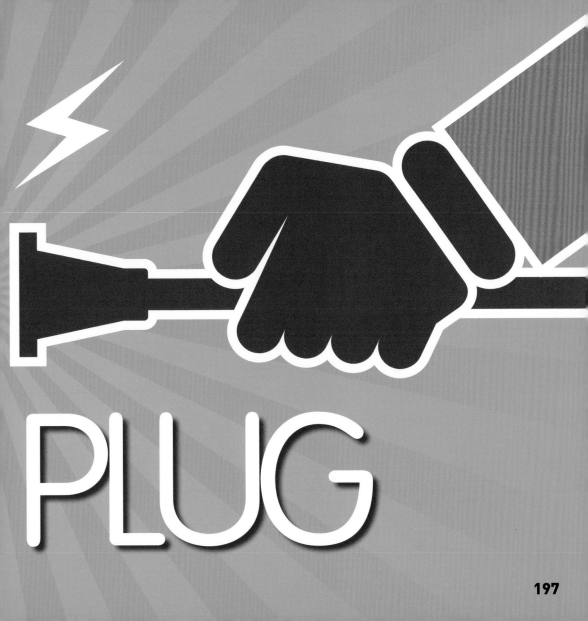

PLUG

TAKE CARE
OF SOMETHING

Whether it be a puppy or a plant, if something relies on you to be there and nurture it, that gives you purpose. And having purpose makes people happy.

79

RECYCLING IS PAW-SOME!

80

A VENDING MACHINE for stray dogs, funded by recycling plastic bottles, was just unveiled in Istanbul, Turkey. When people deposit their plastic bottles into the top of the machine, food for the city's stray dogs is released at the bottom. It encourages people to recycle and it helps out pups in need.

WIN-WIN!

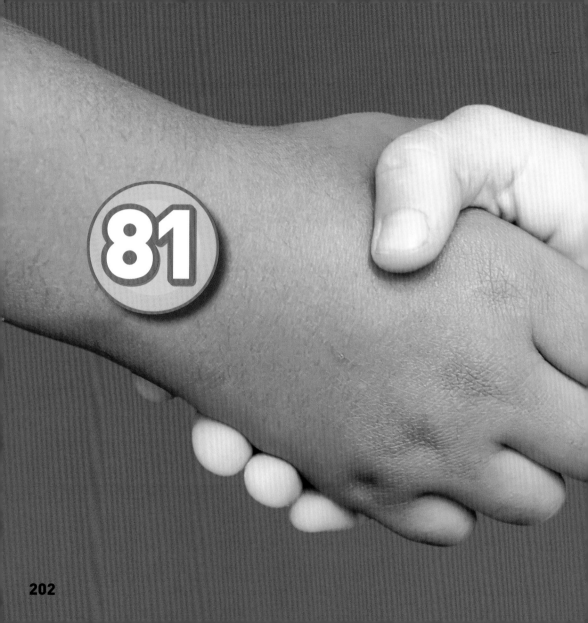

Practice meeting new people and making new friends

FRIENDS ARE THE BEST!

They lift our spirits when we feel down, they encourage us to try new things, and they're superfun to be around. "Studies have shown that the more you surround yourself with people, the happier you tend to be," says Piera Palazzolo, senior vice president at Dale Carnegie Training, a company founded on Dale Carnegie's best-selling book *How to Win Friends and Influence People*. "Friends can be a great source of strength for you, in good times and in bad times."

HERE, PIERA SHARES FIVE TIPS ON HOW TO MAKE LASTING AND MEANINGFUL FRIENDSHIPS.

1 **SHOW GENUINE INTEREST IN OTHERS.** Being a good listener is the most important skill for making new friends. When you first meet someone, aim to spend more time listening than talking about yourself. To do that, all you have to do is ask questions. Do you play any sports? What kinds of music do you listen to? What do you usually do after school? By asking questions rather than talking about yourself, you're showing that you are interested in the other person and what they have to say.

FRIENDSHIP DAY

HAPPY FRIENDSHIP DAY

2 **REMEMBER THEIR NAME.** Dale Carnegie said, "A person's name, to that person, is the sweetest and most important sound in any language." So, when you **first meet someone,** make a mental note of their name and say their name as you speak to them. If you have trouble remembering names, repeat it to yourself when you first hear it. Then try to think of a word, or even someone else's name, that sounds similar.

3 **REMEMBER THE THINGS THAT ARE IMPORTANT TO THEM.** Make a mental note when someone tells you something important that's going on, or coming up, and **follow up with them** about it later. For example, if they have a big test on Wednesday morning, be sure to ask them how it went that afternoon.

4 **SMILE.** This is basic, but often people forget to do it. When you smile, it shows people that you are approachable and that you have **a positive attitude.** Smiling is the first step toward a happy attitude. Dale Carnegie said, "Act enthusiastic and you'll be enthusiastic."

5 **SAY "THANK YOU."** Often people forget to say it, but letting someone know that **you appreciate what they've done for you** is very powerful. If someone helps you with your homework, or lets you borrow their comic book, remember to acknowledge their kindness with a simple "Thank you."

 Research has found that having friends provides all sorts of health benefits, like lowering stress, decreasing the risk of heart disease, and even improving sleep.

GIVE

or treats you badly, it can be hard to move forward. But holding on to that anger and bitterness is actually hurting *you*, not them. And studies have found that forgiving someone can reduce depression, anxiety, and anger. So for your health and happiness, learn to let go and forgive.

"Love is the only force capable of transforming an enemy into a friend." – Martin Luther King, Jr.

discover

SOME

THING 83

No matter how **big** or **small** the discovery may be, if you go looking for **answers** and find them, it's a personal victory. Jack Andraka, **NG emerging explorer,** teen scientist, and author of *BREAKTHROUGH: How One Teen Innovator Is Changing the World,* made a discovery, and his was definitely of the big variety. In fact, **it's pretty huge.**

"Every great dream begins with a dreamer. Always remember, you have within you the strength, the patience, and the passion to reach for the stars to change the world." – Harriet Tubman

WHEN JACK WAS JUST 15, HE INVENTED A NEW TEST FOR DETECTING PANCREATIC, LUNG, AND OVARIAN CANCERS. AND ONE OF THE MOST AMAZING THINGS ABOUT JACK'S TEST IS THAT IT WILL BE ABLE TO DETECT CANCERS AT EARLIER STAGES, WHEN THERE IS A GREATER POSSIBILITY OF A CURE.

An Interview With Jack Andraka

Q: What inspired you to look for a new test for pancreatic cancer?

A: When I was 13 I lost a close family friend, who was like an uncle to me, to pancreatic cancer. It didn't make a lot of sense to me, and I wanted answers.

Q: Did you ever have any doubts that you could do it?

A: I did have doubts, lots of them, but I kept thinking about the one hundred people who die every day from pancreatic cancer. When things got tough, I thought of them.

Q: What do you find fascinating about science?

A: I look at science as trying to solve the mysteries of the universe. What isn't fascinating about that?

Q: What advice would you give to a young person interested in science?

A: Dream big but start slow. When I was a kid, I began with simple experiments, like measuring how many books I could place on top of an egg before the egg would crack. Little experiments like that allowed me to build on my knowledge as I moved on to bigger and more difficult tasks. Just don't stop pushing yourself. All of us are capable of doing really amazing things. If we believe in ourselves, are determined—and have decent Wi-Fi access—anything is possible!

INSTA-SMILE Check out five of the **world's tiniest**

WHAT: World's smallest elephant

WHO: Borneo pygmy elephant

WHY THEY'LL MAKE YOU HAPPY: These elephants are a subspecies of the Asian elephant. Though they're still big animals (the smallest measure about 4 feet 11 inches/150 cm, and their average weight is 2,500 pounds/1,134 kg), their oversize ears and long trunks make them particularly lovable.

84

WHAT: World's smallest deer
WHO: Pudú deer
WHY THEY'LL MAKE YOU HAPPY:
This endangered species lives in South America and ranges from 13 to 17 inches (33–43 cm) tall.

—and cutest!—creatures.

WHAT: World's smallest living dog
WHO: Miracle Milly
WHY SHE'LL MAKE YOU HAPPY:
She is a Chihuahua living in Puerto Rico, and she is about 3.8 inches tall and weighs about 1 pound. When she was born, she could fit in a teaspoon.
(9.7 cm)
(453 g)

WHO: World's smallest bird
WHAT: Bee hummingbird
WHY THEY'LL MAKE YOU HAPPY:
They live in Cuba and the Isle of Youth and are about 2.2 inches long and weigh about 0.06 ounces.
(5.7 cm)
(1.7 g)

WHAT: World's smallest amphibians
WHO: Brazilian gold frog (Brazil) and Monte Iberia eleuth (Cuba)
WHY THEY'LL MAKE YOU HAPPY:
These frogs only grow to be about 0.4 inches long, which is about the length of a housefly.
(1 cm)

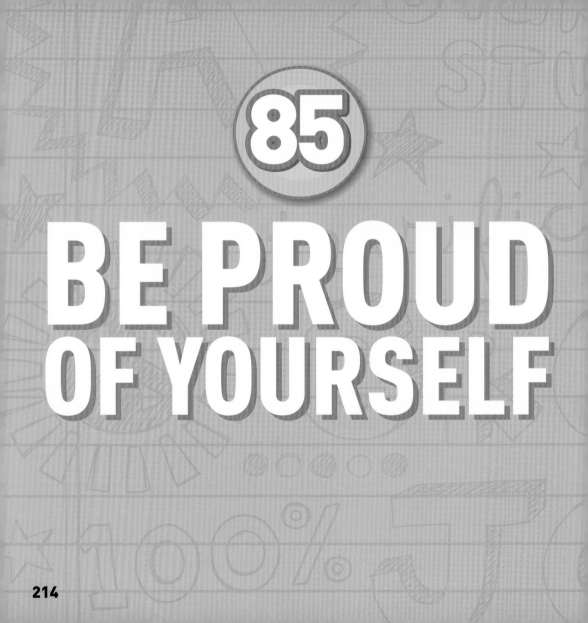

85
BE PROUD OF YOURSELF

(DO THE RIGHT THING, EVEN WHEN IT'S HARD)

86

READ

Visit faraway places, explore magical worlds, and meet amazing new people, all without leaving the couch.

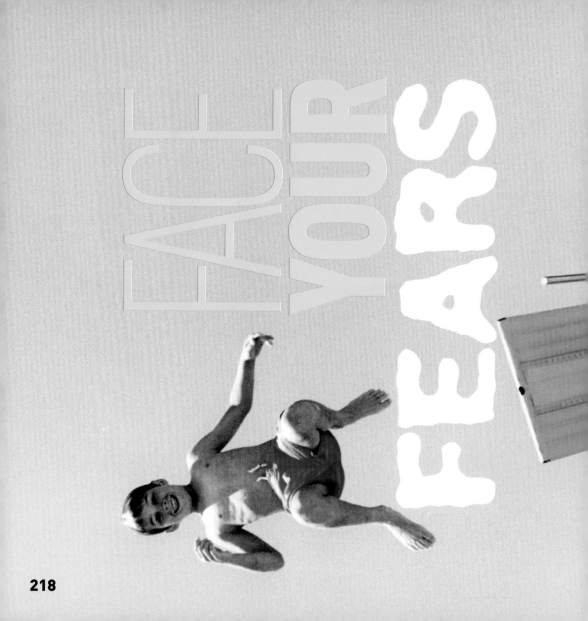

FACE YOUR FEARS

87

"I learned that courage was not the absence of fear, but the triumph over it ... The brave man is not he who does not feel afraid, but he who conquers that fear." – Nelson Mandela

They really

do love us!

A RECENT STUDY SHOWS THAT DOGS AND CATS EXPERIENCE THE SAME LOVE FEELINGS AS HUMANS.

COLLECT MORE EXPERIENCES, LESS STUFF

89

90

Dri
lots of

nk
water

PRACTICE
MINDFULNESS

MINDFULNESS IS A WAY OF EXERCISING AND STRENGTHENING YOUR MIND IN ORDER TO FOCUS ON THE PRESENT. To do this, we direct our attention to something specific, like a sound, smell, or our breath. Focusing on one thing helps quiet our swirling thoughts and create calmness and clarity. "If we're thinking about the past or the future, it's harder to be filled with a sense of happiness," says mindfulness expert and leadership consultant Laurie Cameron. "The number one way mindfulness leads to happiness is that it helps us to savor life in the here and now."

91

SET A GOAL TO PRACTICE MINDFULNESS FOR A FEW MINUTES EVERY DAY.
You can also practice as needed when you feel overwhelmed, stressed, or nervous. Here, Laurie shares three activities that promote mindfulness.

HAPPY ACTIVITY 1: Make a Mindfulness Jar

YOU'LL NEED: 1 clear glass jar with lid, water, 5 drops of glycerin, glitter
DIRECTIONS: Fill the jar with water and add glycerin and glitter. Whenever you feel anxious or overwhelmed, shake your mindfulness jar and set it down in front of you. Watch the swirling glitter and focus your attention on it as it drifts to the bottom of the jar. Take slow, calm breaths, and just like the glitter, your mind will begin to settle.

HAPPY ACTIVITY 2: Go for a Mindfulness Walk

Take a walk through your neighborhood, or even throughout your house, and focus on just one of your senses, like what you're hearing or what you smell. Whenever your mind begins to wander, bring your attention back to that sense. For example, if you're focusing on your sense of smell, what are all of the smells you notice as you walk around your neighborhood? Maybe you smell honeysuckle, or someone grilling in their backyard. Perhaps you smell gasoline from a neighbor's lawnmower, or the soap someone's using to wash their car. Each time you begin to think about school, friends, or family, bring your attention back to these smells. Paying attention, on purpose, to the here and now is how you practice mindfulness.

HAPPY ACTIVITY 3: Do the Stoplight Exercise

HOW TO: When you experience a strong emotion, picture a stoplight. Whether you're scared, stressed, or your feelings are hurt, it's helpful to be able to identify what it is that you're feeling—and practicing mindfulness helps people do that. This exercise is very powerful because it helps you move forward in a more purposeful way when you're experiencing strong emotions, allowing you to become a master of your own thoughts and body.

Step 1:
When you recognize feelings of stress, sadness, or anxiety, **stop.**

Step 2:
Next, slow down and take some **deep, easy breaths.** This is working to calm your nervous system. Focus on sending your breath down to where your feet meet the ground. Do this for one to two minutes.

Step 3:
Now that you've taken a brief **pause to calm down,** you're better able to choose how you want to respond instead of just reacting to your strong feelings.

INSTA-SMILE

92

Micheal Jackson does his signature moonwalk.

A DANCE INSTRUCTOR IN GERMANY PERFORMED THE LONGEST CONTINUOUS MOONWALK BY MOONWALKING FOR MORE THAN TWO AND A HALF HOURS!

93

Be
posi

tive!

SAVOR ALL THAT'S GOOD IN YOUR DAY

Ofer Leidner is the co-founder of the app Happify, which was created based on the science of happiness and positive psychology. Savoring is one of the five main skills that Happify highlights, based on its proven effect on happiness. Here, Ofer highlights three ways someone can practice savoring.

Q: What is savoring and how does it relate to happiness?

A: Savoring is about noticing the good around you and really taking time to prolong and intensify your enjoyment in the moment. It's all about making pleasurable experiences last as long as possible. If you can heighten your awareness and focus on that pleasurable experience, it actually rewires pathways in your brain, activating areas that are associated with happiness. Some of the benefits of savoring include increased optimism as well as reduced stress.

Happy Activity 1: The next time something good happens at school, pay attention. If your teacher gives you a compliment, or your sports team wins a game, take time to let the experience sink in. To prolong the joy, try journaling about the positive experience or sharing the news with someone else.

Happy Activity 2: When you eat a delicious cupcake—or even drink a glass of water—pause and notice the flavors and the texture. Mindfully think of what of it tastes like, and take a moment to be present and appreciate the experience.

Happy Activity 3: Take a walk and savor something that you normally pass by without noticing. Pay attention to everything that you think is beautiful. Look at the architecture, the flowers, and the beautiful stones in the walkway. We often go about our day without noticing, but today, make it a priority to appreciate the beauty around you.

visit the beach,

mountains,
or a waterfall

95

These environments produce lots of negative ions, which are invisible molecules that when inhaled are thought to lower stress and boost our energy and mood!

96

IN LONDON, A FULLY FUNCTIONING BUS STOP WAS MADE ENTIRELY OUT OF LEGOS.

THE CREATORS USED MORE THAN

100,000 LEGO BRICKS

AND IT TOOK TWO WEEKS TO BUILD.

97

DO

something out of

the ORDINARY

TRUST YOUR INSTINCTS

98

AN INSTINCT IS A LITTLE VOICE, OR A HUNCH, THAT COMES FROM YOUR HEAD AND/OR HEART TO TELL YOU WHETHER YOU'RE ON THE RIGHT PATH. Instincts are feelings, or intuitions, that lead you toward the things you're passionate about and away from the things that aren't good for you.

"Trust yourself. You know more than you think you do."
– Benjamin Spock

Ask for help!

Aww!

A NEWBORN PANDA IS ABOUT THE SIZE OF A STICK OF BUTTER, ROUGHLY 1/900 THE SIZE OF ITS MOM.

100

CHECKLIST

- ☐ Have a belly laugh
- ☐ Get silly
- ☐ Get moving
- ☐ Smile
- ☐ Meditate
- ☐ Keep an open mind
- ☐ Learn to love the way you look
- ☐ Pick flowers
- ☐ Care passionately about something you love
- ☐ Watch your favorite TV show or movie
- ☐ Discover a hobby you love
- ☐ Find a group of people who enjoy doing what you enjoy
- ☐ Get organized
- ☐ Be resilient. Never, ever give up
- ☐ Make a list of things you like about you
- ☐ Help people who need it
- ☐ Embrace your weird
- ☐ Listen to music
- ☐ Express your feelings

- ☐ Talk nicely to yourself
- ☐ Be true to yourself
- ☐ Eat chocolate
- ☐ Play with a puppy
- ☐ Be an awesome teammate
- ☐ Get a goldfish and watch it swim
- ☐ Surround yourself with colors that make you happy
- ☐ Dance in the rain
- ☐ Appreciate simple pleasures
- ☐ Find out what makes you happy
- ☐ Call a friend
- ☐ Be kind to others
- ☐ Set aside family time
- ☐ Put perfect to rest
- ☐ Make your bed
- ☐ Keep a journal
- ☐ Get creative
- ☐ Look at pictures of cute animals
- ☐ Be curious

- ☐ Take a nap
- ☐ Learn a skill
- ☐ Celebrate International Day of Happiness
- ☐ Try yoga
- ☐ Give someone a hug or hold someone's hand
- ☐ Be grateful
- ☐ Be open to new ideas
- ☐ Breathe
- ☐ Go outside
- ☐ Don't be afraid to fail
- ☐ Believe in magic
- ☐ Put on your headphones and take a 10-minute dance break
- ☐ Think happy thoughts
- ☐ Have compassion
- ☐ Become an awesome listener
- ☐ Build something, fix something, or figure something out
- ☐ Try aromatherapy
- ☐ Sleep soundly
- ☐ Try something new
- ☐ Set a goal and make a plan to achieve it
- ☐ Unplug
- ☐ Take care of something
- ☐ Practice meeting new people and making new friends
- ☐ Forgive
- ☐ Discover something
- ☐ Be proud of yourself
- ☐ Read
- ☐ Face your fears
- ☐ Collect more experiences, less stuff
- ☐ Drink lots of water
- ☐ Practice mindfulness
- ☐ Be positive
- ☐ Savor all that's good in your day
- ☐ Visit the beach, mountains, or a waterfall
- ☐ Do something out of the ordinary
- ☐ Trust your instincts
- ☐ Ask for help

INDEX

Boldface indicates
illustrations.

A

Accomplish tasks 116–117,
    116–117
Activities
    movement **12–13**, 12–15, **15**
    new 190, **190–191**
    out of the ordinary 240–
        241, **240–241**
    outside 158–159, **158–159**
Amphibians, smallest 213, **213**
Andraka, Jack **209**, 209–210
Animals
    cute 124, **125**
    feelings 220–221, **220–221**
    friendships 38–41, **38–41**
    tiniest 212–213, **212–213**
Appearance 28–31, **29**
Aromatherapy 186–187,
    186–187
Art projects 109, **120–121**, 121

B

Baths 98, **98–99**
Beaches 236
Bed, making yours 116–117,
    116–117
Bee hummingbird 213, **213**
Bicycles **26–27**, 27

Birds, smallest 213, **213**
Body image 28–31, **29**
Breathing **154–155**, 154–157
Bubble baths 98, **98–99**
Build something 182–183,
    182–183

C

Calendars 53
Call a friend 102, **103**
Cameron, Laurie 227–229, **228**
Care for something **198–199**,
    199
Carnegie, Dale 204–205
Cats
    cat cafés **122–123**, 123
    feelings 220–221, **220–221**
    friendship with orangutan
        39, **39**
Celebrations **136–137**, 137
Chicks 78–79, **78–79**
Chimpanzees 150–151, **150–151**
Chocolate 80–83, **80–83**
Chopra, Deepak 20
Cinnamon 187, **187**
Coin from ear (magic trick)
    168–169, **168–169**
Colors 92–93, **92–93**
Compassion 176–177, **176–177**
    be kind to others 106–109,
        106–109
    help people 60–61, **60–61**,
        184, **185**
    keep an open mind 24, **25**

Creativity **120–121**, 121
Curiosity 126–129, **126–129**
Cute animals 124, **125**

D

Dance
    dance break 170, **170–171**
    moonwalk 230–231,
        230–231
    in the rain 94, **94–95**
Deer 38, **38**, 212, **212**
Delgado, Janna 140–141,
    156–157
Discover something **208–
    209**, 208–211, **209**
Do the right thing 215
Dogs
    animal friendships 38,
        38, 41, **41**
    fastest on two legs
        68–69, **68–69**
    feelings 220–221,
        220–221
    hotel shaped like 142, **143**
    play with a puppy 84–85,
        84–85
    recycling to feed stray
        dogs **200–201**, 201
    scuba diving 88, **88–89**
    super pups 58–59, **58–59**
    world's smallest 213, **213**
Drink water 224–225,
    224–225
Ducks 41, **41**

E

Edison, Thomas 163
Elephants
building shaped like 143,
143
friendship with dog 38, **38**
showing compassion 176–
177, **176–177**
smallest 212, **212**
Endorphins 15, 83
Experience things 222,
222–223
Express your feelings **70–71**, 71

F

Failure, fear of **160–161**,
161–163
Family
family time 110, **110–111**
siblings 78–79, **78–79**, 104,
104–105
Fear, facing 218–219, **218–219**
Feelings
in animals 220–221,
220–221
expressing them **70–71**, 71
trust your instincts 242,
242–243
Figure something out 182–183,
182–183
Fish, taking for a walk **164–
165**, 165
Fix something 182–183,
182–183

Flowers 32–33, **32–33**
Food
chocolate 80–83, **80–83**
get creative 121
gingerbread houses 48,
48–49
Forgiveness **206**, 206–207
Friendships
animal friendships 38–41,
38–41
call a friend 102, **103**
kindness club 109
making new friends **202–
203**, 203–205
with oneself 74
shared interests 46–47,
46–47
Frogs, smallest 213, **213**

G

Gingerbread houses 48, **48–49**
Goal-setting 194–195
Goldfish 90, **90–91**
Goldsmith, Greg **128**, 128–129
Gorillas **175**
Grass 187, **187**
Gratitude 146–149, **147**, 205

H

Hands, holding 144–145,
144–145
Happify app 235
Happy list 100–101, **100–101**
Happy thoughts **172–173**, 173

Help, asking for **244–245**,
245
Helping others
buy lunch 184, **184–185**
people in need 60–61,
60–61
Hobbies 44, **44–45**, 46–47,
46–47
Hold hands 144–145,
144–145
Hugging 144–145
Hummingbirds 213, **213**

I

Ideas 152, **152–153**
Instincts 242, **242–243**
Interests, shared 46–47,
46–47
International Day of
Happiness **136–137**, 137

J

Jackson, Michael **230**
Jenkins, Kathy 51–53
Jokes 8–9
Journals 118–119, 149

K

Kindness
be kind to others 106–
109, **106–109**
help people 60–61,
60–61, 184, **185**
keep an open mind 24, **25**

251

Kindness (cont.)
show compassion 176–177, **176–177**
Kite, Lindsay 30

L

Laughter 6
Lavender 187, **187**
Learn a skill 134–135, **134–135**
Legos 238–239, **238–239**
Lender, Ofer 235
Lemons 187, **187**
Listening **178–179,** 179–181, 204

M

Magic 166–169, **166–169**
Marine biology 36–37
Masland, Dash **36,** 36–37
McCauley, Chris 167
McRaven, William H. 116
Meditation **20–21,** 20–23
Mindfulness **226–227,** 227–229, 235
Miniature horses 192–193, **192–193**
Monk seals 37
Moonwalk (dance) 230–231, **230–231**
Mountains 236
Movement **12–13,** 12–15
Movies 42–43, **42–43**
Music 64–67, **64–67,** 71

N

Naps 130, **130–131**
New activities 190, **190–191**

O

Open-mindedness 24, **25,** 152, **152–153**
Orangutans 39, **39**
Organization 50–53, **50–53,** 116–117, **116–117**
Otters **16–17,** 17
Outside activities 158–159, **158–159**
Owls **174**
Oxytocin 145

P

Palazzolo, Piera 204–205
Pandas 246–247, **246–247**
Papers, organizing 53
Passion **34–35,** 34–37, **36,** 44, **44–45**
Penguins **174**
Perfection 112–113
Perry, Katy 162
Pet fish **164–165,** 165
Pigs 40, **40**
Play
activities **12–13,** 12–15, **15**
with a puppy 84–85, **84–85**
silliness **10,** 11, **11**

Positive attitude 205, 232–235, **232–235**
Pride 214–215
Purpose, sense of **198–199,** 199

R

Rabbits 38, **38,** 132–133, **132–133,** 167
Rain, dancing in 94, **94–95**
Reading **216–217,** 217
Recycling **200–201,** 201
Resilience 54–55, **54–55**
Riddles 8–9
Roller coasters **26–27,** 27
Rowling, J. K. 163

S

Savoring 235
Schonert-Reichl, Kimberly A. 108
Scuba diving 88, **88–89**
Seahorses 96, **96–97**
Sea otters **16–17,** 17
Seals 37
Self image
be proud 214–215
be true to yourself 76, **76–77**
body image 28–31, **29**
embrace your weird 62–63, **62–63**
feelings **70–71,** 71
happy list 100–101, **100–101**

talk nicely to yourself 72–75, **72–75**
things you like about you 56–57, **56–57**
Self-talk 72–75, **72–75**
Service animals 192–193, **192–193**
Shared interests 46–47, **46–47**
Siblings 78–79, **78–79**, 104, **104–105**
Silliness **10**, 11, **11**
Simple pleasures 98, **98–99**
Skills, learning 134–135, **134–135**
Sky Cycle roller coaster **26–27**, 27
Sleep 130, **130–131**, 188–189, **188–189**
Smiling **18–19**, 19, 205
Snowboarding **12–13**
Snow sculptures **104–105**
Spielberg, Steven 162
Sports 86–87, **86–87**
Squirrels 114, **114–115**
Stone, Emma 62
Stress relief 156
Success after failure 162–163

T

Take care of something **198–199**, 199
Talking 71, 72–75, **72–75**
Tasks, accomplishing 116–117, **116–117**
Team sports 86–87, **86–87**
Television 42–43, **42–43**
Thankfulness 146–149, **147**, 205
Think happy thoughts **172–173**, 173
Tickled animals 174–175, **174–175**
Tigers 40, **40**
Tiniest animals 212–213, **212–213**
Touch, power of 144–145, **144–145**
Travel 142, **142–143**, 236–237, **236–237**
Tropical ecology 128–129, **128–129**
Try something new 190, **190–191**
TV shows 42–43, **42–43**

U

Unplug 196–197, **196–197**

V

Vacations 142, **142–143**, 236–237, **236–237**
Vanilla 187, **187**
Volunteer 61

W

Water, drinking 224–225, **224–225**
Waterfalls 236, **236–237**
Weirdness 62–63, **62–63**
Wilson, Angela 140–141
Winfrey, Oprah 163
Wright, Angela 93
Writing
  express your feelings 71
  get creative 121
  gratitude journal 149
  keep a journal 118–119
  kindness log 108
  thank-you notes 149

Y

Yoga 138–141, **138–141**

Find Out More

Grab a parent and discover even more insta-smiles by going online to **kids.nationalgeographic.com** or by going to **natgeo.com/kids/happy**.

PHOTO CREDITS

120, PLAINVIEW/Getty Images; 122 (LE), Lena Ivanova/SS; 122–123, AFP/Getty Images; 123 (RT), Borkin Vadim/SS; 125 (UPLE), IS; 125 (CTR LE), L.F/SS; 125 (LOLE), amrishw/SS; 125 (UPRT), Vishnevskiy Vasily/SS; 125 (CTR RT), IS; 125 (LORT), Vladimir Melnik/SS; 126–127, Enrico Fianchini/Getty Images; 128, courtesy Greg Goldsmith; 129, bluehand/SS; 130–131, Thomas Grass/Getty Images; 132–133, Jiang Hongyan/SS; 134 (UPLE), artemisphoto/SS; 134 (UPRT), PhotoTerry J Alcorn, Inc.grapher/IS; 134 (LOLE), Khakimullin Aleksandr/SS; 134 (LO CTR), EpicStockMedia/SS; 134 (LORT), Artush/SS; 135 (UPLE), Iakov Filimonov/SS; 135 (UP CTR), Ben Schonewille/SS; 135 (UPRT), racorn/SS; 135 (LOLE), Coffee Lover/SS; 135 (LO CTR), Air Images/SS; 135 (LORT), George Nazmi Bebawi/SS; 136–137, Flickr RF/Getty Images; 138–139, Ivory27/SS; 140–141, SS; 142, Andre Jenny/Alamy; 143 (LE), M&N/Alamy; 143 (RT), Franck Fotos/Alamy; 144–145, Zurijeta/SS; 147, age fotostock RM/Getty Images; 150, Anup Shah/Getty Images; 151, Martin Harvey/Alamy; 152–153, SS; 154–155, Vetta/Getty Images; 158–159,

Smith Collection/Getty Images; 160–161, Daniel Milchev/Getty Images; 164–165, Mercury Press/Caters News Agency; 166–167 (BACK), SS; 166–167, Ljupco Smokovski/SS; 168–169 (BACK), SS; 168 (UP), Asaf Eliason/SS; 169 (ALL), Rebecca Hale, NGS; 170–171, Yuri Arcurs/IS; 172, SS; 174 (LE), Ingo Arndt/Minden Pictures; 174 (RT), James.Pintar/SS; 175, IS; 176–177, Johan Swanepoel/SS; 178, Voronin76/SS; 182–183, alphaspirit/SS; 184 (LE), Melpomene/SS; 184 (BACK), K Woodgyer/SS; 185 (BOTH), courtesy Amber Taipalus; 186 (LE), nito/SS; 186 (RT), baibaz/SS; 187 (UPLE), Subbotina Anna/SS; 187 (CTR RT), Viktar Malyshchyts/SS; 187 (LO), antpkr/SS; 188–189, SS; 190–191, Luis Louro/SS; 192, Kristan Lieb/Getty Images; 193, Juniors Bildarchiv GmbH/Alamy; 194, SS; 195, SS; 196–197, SS; 198–199, Ariel Skelley/Getty Images; 200, Amy Rene/SS; 201, worker/SS; 202–203, Mariia Masich/SS; 204, SS; 206–207, Yury Zap/Alamy; 208 (UPLE), Caiaimage/Paul Bradbury/Getty Images; 208 (UPRT), Design Pics RF/Getty Images; 208 (LOLE), Muriel de Seze/Getty Images; 208 (LORT), Mieke Dalle/Getty Images; 209 (UPLE), Aurora

Open/Getty Images; 209 (UPRT), National Geographic Creative/Getty Images; 209 (LOLE), AE Pictures Inc./Getty Images; 209 (LORT), Johner Images/Getty Images; 210, Mark Tucker; 212 (LE), Suzi Eszterhas/Minden Pictures; 212 (RT), Warwick Sloss/ npl/Minden Pictures; 213 (UPLE), Tom Vezo/Minden Pictures; 213 (UPRT), WENN/Newscom; 213 (LO), Steve Winter/National Geographic Creative; 214–215, SS; 216, pau-laphoto/SS; 218–219, Joe McBride/Getty Images; 220, IS; 221, IS; 222–223, Flickr RF/Getty Images; 224–225, Mario7/SS; 226–227, Ghislain & Marie David de Lossy/Getty Images; 228, courtesy Dr. Laurie Cameron; 230, Redferns/Getty Images; 231, Getty Images; 232–233, Markus Gann/SS; 234–235, Mandy Godbehear/SS; 236–237, Flickr RM/Getty Images; 238, AP Images/Paul Brown/REX; 239, AP Images/Anthony Devlin; 240–241, Gideon Hart/Getty Images; 243, AE Pictures Inc./Getty Images; 244–245, PhotoAlto/Getty Images; 246, Katherine Feng/ Globio/Minden Pictures; 247, Katherine Feng/Globio/Minden Pictures

For Abigail and Andy, the brightest of lights, who make me the happiest. –LG

STAFF FOR THIS BOOK
Ariane Szu-Tu, *Project Editor*
Julide Dengel, *Art Director and Designer*
Hillary Leo, *Photo Editor*
Paige Towler, *Editorial Assistant*
Sanjida Rashid and Rachel Kenny, *Design Production Assistants*
Michael Cassady, *Rights Clearance Specialist*
Grace Hill, *Managing Editor*
Michael O'Connor, *Production Editor*
Lewis R. Bassford, *Production Manager*
Jennifer Hoff, *Manager, Production Services*
Susan Borke, *Legal and Business Affairs*
Rebekah Cain, *Imaging Technician*

PUBLISHED BY THE NATIONAL GEOGRAPHIC SOCIETY
Gary E. Knell, *President and CEO*
John M. Fahey, *Chairman of the Board*
Melina Gerosa Bellows, *Chief Education Officer*
Declan Moore, *Chief Media Officer*
Hector Sierra, *Senior Vice President and General Manager, Book Division*

Senior Management Team, Kids Publishing and Media
Nancy Laties Feresten, *Senior Vice President;* Jennifer Emmett, *Vice President, Editorial Director, Kids Books;* Julie Vosburgh Agnone, *Vice President, Editorial Operations;* Rachel Buchholz, *Editor and Vice President,* NG Kids *magazine;* Michelle Sullivan, *Vice President, Kids Digital;* Eva Absher-Schantz, *Design Director;* Jay Sumner, *Photo Director;* Hannah August, *Marketing Director;* R. Gary Colbert, *Production Director*

Digital Anne McCormack, *Director;* Laura Goertzel, Sara Zeglin, *Producers;* Jed Winer, *Special Projects Assistant;* Emma Rigney, *Creative Producer;* Brian Ford, *Video Producer;* Bianca Bowman, *Assistant Producer;* Natalie Jones, *Senior Product Manager*

DISCLAIMER
Neither the publisher nor the author shall be liable for any bodily harm that may be caused or sustained as a result of conducting any of the activities described in this book.

The National Geographic Society is one of the world's largest nonprofit scientific and educational organizations. Founded in 1888 to "increase and diffuse geographic knowledge," the Society's mission is to inspire people to care about the planet. It reaches more than 400 million people worldwide each month through its official journal, *National Geographic,* and other magazines; National Geographic Channel; television documentaries; music; radio; films; books; DVDs; maps; exhibitions; live events; school publishing programs; interactive media; and merchandise. National Geographic has funded more than 10,000 scientific research, conservation, and exploration projects and supports an education program promoting geographic literacy.

For more information, please visit nationalgeographic.com, call 1-800-NGS LINE (647-5463), or write to the following address:
National Geographic Society
1145 17th Street N.W.
Washington, D.C. 20036-4688 U.S.A.

Visit us online at nationalgeographic.com/books

For librarians and teachers: ngchildrensbooks.org

More for kids from National Geographic:
kids.nationalgeographic.com

For information about special discounts for bulk purchases, please contact National Geographic Books Special Sales: ngspecsales@ngs.org

For rights or permissions inquiries, please contact National Geographic Books Subsidiary Rights: ngbookrights@ngs.org

Library of Congress Cataloging-in-Publication Data

Gerry, Lisa.
   100 things to make you happy / by Lisa M. Gerry.
      pages cm
   Includes index.
   ISBN 978-1-4263-2058-3 (pbk. : alk. paper) -- ISBN 978-1-4263-2059-0 (reinforced library binding : alk. paper)
   1. Happiness in children--Juvenile literature. 2. Happiness--Juvenile literature. I. Title. II. Title: One hundred things to make you happy.
   BF723.H37G47 2015
   081--dc23
                                        2014036169

Printed in China
15/RRDS/1

Topsy + Tim

go to hospital

Jean and Gareth Adamson

PUFFIN BOOKS

PUFFIN BOOKS

Published by the Penguin Group
Penguin Books Ltd, 27 Wrights Lane, London W8 5TZ, England
Penguin Books USA Inc., 375 Hudson Street, New York, NY 10014, USA
Penguin Books Australia Ltd, Ringwood, Victoria, Australia
Penguin Books Canada Ltd, 10 Alcorn Avenue, Toronto, Ontario, Canada M4V 3B2
Penguin Books (NZ) Ltd, 182–190 Wairau Road, Auckland 10, New Zealand

Penguin Books Ltd, Registered Offices: Harmondsworth, Middlesex, England

First published by Blackie Children's Books 1994
Reissued in Puffin Books 1996
1 3 5 7 9 10 8 6 4 2

Made and printed in Great Britain by William Clowes Limited, Beccles and London

Tim was going to hospital.
He had fallen out of a tree
and bumped his head.
Topsy and Mummy helped Tim
to pack the things he would need
in hospital.

The hospital was very big,
with bedrooms called wards.
One ward had funny pictures
on the walls.
'This must be the children's ward,'
said Mummy.
A nurse called Sister helped Tim
put his things away in his own
special locker.

'The porter will take you to be
photographed in a minute,' said Sister.
'It will be an X-ray photograph—
the kind that shows what you
look like inside.'

The porter came,
pushing a big
wheelchair for Tim
to sit in.
'Can Mummy come
too?' asked Tim.
'Of course she can,'
said Sister.

It was a long way to the X-ray room.
Tim enjoyed his wheelchair ride.

He saw another porter pushing a
little girl along. She waved to Tim
as they passed.

The lady who worked the X-ray camera stood behind a screen. She could see Tim through a little window.

Mummy stayed with Tim but she
had to wear a special apron.
The X-ray photograph was soon taken.

After lunch, the children went to bed.
Mummy tucked Tim in.
'Now I must go home to look after
Topsy,' she said. 'But don't worry,
I'll soon be back.'

'Bring Topsy with you,' said Tim.
'I will,' said Mummy, but Tim
didn't hear. He was already
fast asleep.

Topsy brought her best jigsaw puzzle
when she came to see Tim in hospital.
She thought he would like to play
with it in bed.

Tim was not in bed. He was playing with the other children.

He took Topsy to meet his new friends.

On the way home, Topsy told Mummy she had a pain—but she was not sure where it was. Mummy did not believe her.

'I want to go to hospital too,' said Topsy.

'Cheer up, Topsy,' said Dad, when
he came home from work. 'I've brought
a surprise present for you.'

The surprise present was a medical set
with a syringe, a stethoscope and a
thermometer.

When Topsy came home from school
next day, she found Tim waiting
for her.
'Mummy brought me home,' said Tim.
'My head's all right now.'

Soon every toy in the house was in
Topsy and Tim's children's hospital.